the day barque

A REVIEW OF POETRY, PROSE AND THE ARTS

APOLLO POETRY SOCIETY

The Day Barque

A review of poetry, prose and the arts

Volume 2, Number 1

July 2014

The Day Barque

A review of poetry, prose and the arts

Published by Apollo Poetry Society

P. O. Box 716, Oregon House, CA 95962

Volume 2, Number 1

Cover: *On the Beach* by Carol Davis

Editors: Judith Grace, Stefano Petrizzo

Design and Production: Margaret Jean Campbell

Visit www. thedaybarque.com

This book is set in Adobe Caslon Type Text.

Printed in the United States of America

Volume 1, Number 1: December 2013

Volume 2, Number 1: July 2014

ISBN-13:978-0692242056

ISBN-10:0692242058

1. Poetry 2. Art 3. Literature 4. Spirituality

Volume 2, Number 1

July 2014

CONTENTS

ARTISTS

APOLLO POETRY SOCIETY

Jo Anna Mortensen

The Great Land

I want to hide between the wind's fingers.
I want that vast turquoise lake to thirst for my return.
I want to catch up on the fireweed's gossip
and search the dall sheep's gaze for secrets.

That the child may wander without betraying
the name of her creamy-barked birch;
that she will be awake first and her bare feet
memorize pebbles and the cool licks of waves.

Can you see fog coveting morning's colors
scheming to pocket the lake's beauty?
Sunlight rebuffs this mischief;
whips violet and gold across the water.

But do not wake the stranger sleeping on ferns
or let the vole strip bark from the birch;
nudge me if the Great One appears
sobering, shattering, immense in the midnight sun.

Magic Carpet   Linda Carter Holman

Jo Anna Mortensen

The Ventilator
for Nori

The Day Nurse:

It's an incredible invention, the ventilator, a lifesaving wizard.
My fingers know now how to insert the plastic tubes,
without scratching the nasal passages and trachea.
This patient held still, lucid and uncomplaining,
while her large green eyes watched me, flashing trust and fear,
like a railroad-crossing warning light.

The Doctor:

The ventilator buys time, so I can watch the signs.
The pneumonia's receding; I like her breathing—
perhaps she's pulling through.
We'll take it out tomorrow; fingers crossed.
Once it's out; I'm not signing off on an order to reinsert.

The Daughter:

Her body heaves as she gasps for air,
making the tubes tremble in her nostrils.
Seeing her fine features broken up and twisted
by strange plastic patches and skinny cylinders
reminds me of a face from Picasso's painting, *Guernica*,
beauty colliding with the horror of war.
Here the brutal battle is within her body.

The Patient:

Night is coming and my children will leave soon.
Bedding down with a ventilator scares me.
It's calming to watch the silent snow make falling look easy.
This is the first time I've wondered if
death will be fun.

Death:

The ventilator is only a pawn,
positioned to protect this patient,
because there are no other pieces to play with.
I know my moves, which are always unhurried,
even when they appear swift in the realm of men.
I bear no grudges.
Checkmate is exactly four days away.

The Ventilator:

Sometimes it is hours, sometimes days, never long—
my time inside the body,
blowing oxygen breath by breath, keeping the heart beating.
Still, the work is monotonous;
I dream that I'm a small boy's toy.
He puts me in his pocket, takes me to the creek
and begins engineering experiments.
Awake, I yearn to hear gurgling waters,
wind in the pines and
the airy voice of a child without cares.

Jo Anna Mortensen

The Absolute Atheist

Death came for me in the early morning
with that good-looking night nurse Nate holding my hand
you arrived
stunned
too late for my last breath
kissed my cooling cheek
wished me well on the journey
that Aunt Reva always called going over the hump
humbling for me having preached oblivion
to find myself shifting into a subtler shape
others here are helping me
me an absolute atheist
still I'm yearning to yank your hair or yodel
it galls me
that you're not noticing
since only you, my wayward daughter,
and Grandma Doe called me out on my bleak afterlife predictions
she's helping me now
also you badgered me until we finally made a pact
lightly laughing but both knowing
we were earnest
tell me if you're wrong you said
your brown eyes grinning
when you're gone
send a sign

I tried delivering on my promise
when you reached the Providence Hospital lobby
I called your name
one syllable
Jo
urgent
you froze
shifted your gaze from lazy snowflakes outside
to scrutinize a handful of strangers
neither the voice of a man or woman
startled you took a second look then moved on
so I tried winging my way
that very morning of my December departure
the first bluebird returned to your apple orchard
sign of happiness a sign
you wondered
waited for me in dreams
then sank into your surprise at sadness
I can save you all that
here—I'm helping you now
place in your shoe
like a tiny smooth pebble
this conviction
of absolute love

Jo Anna Mortensen

Find Me

Through the thin slit, I watch you come by to find me.
That's the game we play, hide-and-seek, try to find me.

Didn't that charismatic carpenter reassure us?
"I won't leave you; search low and high to find me."

We couldn't quite catch Odysseus' words to his wife,
"You've paid with an ocean of sighs to find me."

And wasn't white-haired Walt the poet we all loved?
"…under your boot-soles, by and by… you'll find me."

Hear that chatty cook as he chops leeks for his stew?
"Leap in my pan, sweet onion rings, and fry to find me."

Remember when Beast entered Beauty's dream as a prince?
"Mistrust your eyes; you must doubt my disguise to find me."

Doesn't every mother play peek-a-boo with her cranky baby?
Veil and reveal, "Yoo-hoo! Be clever with your eyes to find me."

Telling God, "If the tiger swallows me, I'll have to go down."
God laughs, "Be swallowed; Josie, be tiger pie to find Me."

Horseback Riding   Deborah McKay

Mark Mitchell   Carol Davis

Mark Mortensen

August

The winds of August
have swept the land again
I do not recognize
many things now

What was once gathered closely
now stands alone
And what could not bend
lies flat and broken

Nearby a women stands in her doorway naked
her now ragged clothes
lie folded at her feet

And beyond a young man
walks the street briskly
Coming out from under
a slow-moving cloud of regret

Still… there is the one
on the rooftop, exposed
Like a Greek statue
Looking out through shafts of eternity
at things he himself is made of

Mark Mortensen

The Swing

There is an oak tree on the path
behind Antonio's garage, huge, ancient
maybe three hundred years old with branches
arching in every direction

This morning a light breeze disturbs
the dry leaves piled beneath it
and a long forgotten swing hanging from
the highest bough sways listlessly
like a silent chime in the wind

From rustling leaves
a faint echo of playful young voices
rises, drifts… and is gone
Transfixed
I say out loud to myself
"I have no home anymore,
not in this world."

John Craig

Petite Wisdoms

XXIII

The miraculous is always mercilessly pursued
by the formatory. The wedding becomes a required
anniversary gift, the birth a cake stuck with candles.
To stay above this quicksand, you must stand still at the speed
of unimpeded nervous light; you must be the miracle
above the associative decoding going on
in your head as your dogged eyes chase this line of letters.

XXXVI

You can root it in your body and hate mortality.
You can funnel it into your children and their children.
You can bestow it on the world in some respected work.
You can invest it in intricate knowledge the world wants.
I speak of identity. You can consolidate it
in a spot on your tie, waste it in independent pride
or return it to the perfect present from which it fell.

XLVIII

Is it worth combing through the wreckage to find the black box
or diving through the layers of memory to locate
the primal trauma? Sometimes the context of ruin we think
will let us understand just deviates us all the more,
and with the torch of a brash new theory, we hurry on
preparing for the past. The soul observes eternity.
Our reserved seats on this crashing plane are but circumstance.

Self–Portrait   Charles Frank

John Craig

The Suitor

"Let me know if your thoughts on this change," he said as he turned
to leave. He was embarrassed, as he had known he would be,
but all in all, the sting of rejection was not as bad
as the imagination of it. The clear, upright part
of him endured, unshaken, stronger for the next advance.
He had spoken honorable feeling with honesty
and modesty. There is no failure in an open heart.

Again and again as half a year passed, he asserted
the ritual pledge. If the first required greatest effort,
The second was most awkward, the closest to collapsing.
By the third time, he was aware of a clear procedure,
a focused intention of language and posture and tone.
She surprised him at the fourth, urging him to give it up,
but he persevered, and the vignette ended smilingly.

By the fifth he was near command, speaking with a calmness
close to certainty. Fixed and reliable, yet gracious
and kind, he was a marvel to her, and though she did not
say yes, yet she could not say no. The sixth visit lasted
all afternoon, and even the silences were fruited
and sweet. Lighting the lamp, she said, "The time does not rule us.
You are not the man I once rejected. Stay here and dine."

John Craig

Love and Children

The hardest thing is to let them explore. Their injuries
will form scars, and the scars become their secret vanities.
Later, if they ask for your instruction, your radiance
must be ready. Now you think you must be their protector,
but in truth you are their first destination of return.
Then and only then, as they limp over the hill and glimpse
the promise of home, can your welcome of love have meaning.

What will their absence teach you? Impotence, humility,
self-forgiveness. The strengthening of true conscience scrapes clean
the cave of your heart then decorates the walls with praising.
No longer is your gaze, which bounds up the hill to the sky,
driven by desire or hope but by readiness to give,
to pour itself into God. Then and only then appear
the still sweet bruised ones who now need you.
Open your poor arms.

A Girl   Genya Gritchin

Self-Portrait   Charles Frank

John Craig

All This

When you've been swallowed, don't lose God. Don't die inside the fish.
Remember Jonah: stay prayerful and firm in the present,
even if everything flooding in from your ruined senses
makes you sick, and your lungs are turning inside out sucking
the unreal air. The lower self waited for you to wade
into the polluted sea then made its move, engulfing
your identity, claiming you completely. Don't die here.

Let your mind scrape the lowest depths of yourself for the will
to utter the soul's simplest command: be. Repeat, repeat
and repeat. Let each formulation of that syllable
be more intentional than the last. Let mindfulness sink
its root into the soft belly of darkness; establish
the real separation. A vague nausea will begin
to trouble the monster. Hold on through its wretching spasms.

And when you are vomited forth—ears ringing, eyes burning—
Onto the shore of the good earth, don't spill your gratitude.
Keep it close. Give it silently to God by focusing
your gaze on a single beautiful thing—a bird or branch—
standing out against the sky. In the full range of being,
you are all this: the temptation, the belly of darkness,
the surviving mind, the will to return, the light of God.

Judith Grace

My Town

My town came out of a man's brow
Bringing gardeners and builders and fresco painters
With his secret waay to turn them around

It brought chefs, many poets, a juggler, a clown
Ministers, bankers, and pastry makers
My town came out of a man's brow

Children came running in costumes and crowns
And dancers on point and mandolin players
With his secret way to turn them around

Camels and ibex rode in from the south
And ostriches, yaks, in the orchards and gardens
My town came out of a man's brow

Twenty-one springs sprang up from the ground
O! and bells there and statues, bright roses and fountains
With his secret way to turn them around

Families and lovers came to my town
And death came too, bringing rivers of sorrows
My town came out of a man's brow
With his secret way to turn them around

Lily   Jonathan Beth

Judith Grace

Prisoner

I never knew I could be happy with myself
All alone in my striped pajamas
Dancing around
Like a prisoner on parole

So that even my dog turns and wonders
Who?

Water Lilies   Larisa Kostyreva

Judith Grace

This Delirium of Blossoms

This delirium of blossoms
Quadrillions of petals dancing cotillions
All the dyes of the rainbow running together
Leafing along the continuum

Quadrillions of petals dancing cotillions
Pistils and stamens unfurling like fireworks
Leafing along the continuum
Odorously blowing over the thorns

Pistils and stamens unfurling like fireworks
Pawning all of my jewels for you
Odorously blowing over the thorns
Mercy all the days of our lives

Pawning all of my jewels for you
This hallelujah of flowers
Mercy all the days of our lives
This delirium of blossoms

Judith Grace

Cranach's *Fountain of Youth*

For weeks the creaking cart loaded with us old
Rolled through the misshapen mountains, the bleached out
Boulders and bushes of thorn. The clouds like grey
Gargoyles hung over us as the cart-horses wheezed.

Arriving at the clearing, at the square marble pool,
They stripped us of our rotting rags. I covered myself
With both my hands, ashamed to show my withered flesh,
And kneeled there, afraid, on the marble's edge…

Dare I step in? I remembered you, all
My bruises and my memories, my broken city.
Would I have to surrender you now?
My scars may be deep, but they are all I possess.

I huddled for many days on that shore
As if I were plunging into the open sea,
Then when I could weep no more, I descended at last
The three smooth stairs, submerging my prayers

I cannot tell you what happened then
In that strange pool fed by the tall narrow fountain
Except that the water was cool and clear
And I bathed there for only an instant

But when I emerged on the other side
Immaculate leaves were covering the trees
And in the garden bespangled with rosebuds
A great table was set out for a feast

Golden Face   Linda Carter Holman

Elegant lovers in bright silken clothes
Were dancing in pairs to a mandolin
On a far high hill a white city shone
And beneficent clouds spun overhead.

I took one last look behind me then entered the tent
That was laid out with fresh clean garments—
But I cannot tell you what was happening then
For from head to toe I was becoming a blossom.

Citrus   Tatyana Holodnova

Judith Grace

Lemon Poem

Blindingly yellow, thick-skinned and lightly pocked
I cut you into two perfect Eyes of Horus
Sun-flecked with golden pulp in which your pale seeds float
What makes you a poem is how much the sun is bursting through your sun

Judith Grace

Stone Buddha

All over the earth, at every moment, someone
is stopping what he is doing.
He is tasting a ripened cherry, slowly closing the pages of his book,
or perhaps seeing birds in V-shaped formation veering against the sky,
Puzzled for a second that it is someone else, not him,
Looking out of his eyes.

Suddenly his ambitions and his plans grow terrifyingly small
And he worries and he wonders
if he has lost some essential coin
that has slipped out of his pocket
Or if he is missing the code, like a semaphore waving in the distance,
which would have kept him from drowning.

All over the earth, for a second,
Someone is realizing that it is You who have always been
Watching and Listening
You have looked out of your infinitely knowing eyes forever
Waiting for the ones who will finally recognize You in the mirror.
Every second someone is praying earnestly to know You—
And then You come.

Ragab   Brian Flynn

Judith Grace

Final Descent

My arms are becoming spirals
A soft rumbling starts inside me: it is my heart
Angels are whispering blessings
Go now and be turned into a crucible and be made one of us
My body-tunic is put on; knotted with the knots I will have to untie
Dyed with the deeds I will need to do; my loves, visions, prayers
They will seem important and make me forget
I will get so much smaller than God, and perhaps will disappear…

I enter the hourglass again, and it is turned…

Shyly, like a rainbow falling to earth, I am
Appearing…
The faces of these exhausted, expectant, radiant strangers are kind
For a moment their masks have cracked open and a flicker of eternity has entered
They have been waiting for me to change their lives, but I am not waiting for
anything…
I already love them…

Now suddenly these great and open hands which hold me release me
Into this vibrating hive of waves, words, shadows, touches, colors, demands…
Falling through the hourglass, back into time
The final descent from the stars begins, and a name comes.

Les Amants   Auguste Haboush

Auguste Haboush

To a Lover

In your arms my life vanished.
In your arms never was loss found again.
In your arms a sword cut a swath of ecstasy,
piercing all boundaries.

Let the imbeciles and moribunds gawk.
Our merging continents hear only the tectonic plates diving
under—slanted slabs jut up till the sky is cut in two.
Our coastlines barely touch and are licked away by a hungry sea.

Secrets fade into the witness protection program as the missing
bodies are swept beneath the wall-to-wall carpet.
In your arms our stolen identities are free to enter
the darkest taverns we choose.

I do not take death threats with a grain of salt,
when wounds like ours remain open to the heart.

Turbaned Man   Auguste Haboush

Auguste Haboush

In Time

My friend—it's not too late to laugh and wait for something sublime.
After all, my dear, what can be worth the risk of losing it in time?

Dreams of a union awake the desire as the dawn chases dusk.
Throw away plans—no warning, you cannot choose it in time.

Why take a shortcut on such a beautiful path to God's paradise?
Every step to heaven is a joy, silly fool—don't peruse it in time.

Birds sing praise, frogs and crickets chant where we are headed.
Come! celebrate and suffer, laugh at your body and abuse it in time.

Darling friend, you and I have grace with all the will of the master.
No one having paid as us and seen the divine would refuse it in time.

Auguste Haboush

Given Away

I have given myself away to you,
offered up this menagerie, this cacophony of
Longings and desires to you—all of it.

I have put myself into your hands, my arms and all that they could carry
Dropped away as far as distance implies.

Given away are the shoes that we
Danced away the night in.

Given away are the clothes you would undress from me.
Given away are the things which stood between us,
Toaster ovens, Frigidaires and stacks of periodicals.

 Given away was the poem you wrote to me by giving it
A title, only to find it after you turned our house on end.

Given away is the grain of sand that stands as a monument to time.
An embryonic pearl in the necklace of the milky way

We are both hanging in the lover's noose that dangles from the crescent moon,
Given over and away from reach of mountain tops.

Self-Portrait   Anthony Emmolo

Albert Gasparian

Odysseus

Once monsters are defeated one by one, just wait,
Don't rush after, catching its glimpse from a distance,
Your staying power takes you to the crossroads.
Slowly, or spontaneously, the situation will change.
Seeing face to face is different—quiet, silent, calm.
Enchanting evening comes and you possess your soul.
United with your island of sanity, the promised land,
Secrets, lies, losses, pains—was it all not worth it?

White Lotus   Brian Flynn

Jane Horton

The Dying Branch

Through the dark tangle of pine and oak
A shaft of light has made its way
And lit upon a broken limb.
Hanging down, almost free of the tree,
Its leaves gone, its web of twig and vines intricate
Almost ornamental.

The details are picked out by light and shadow,
Bright and dark,
Like a Rembrandt painting of a Celtic brooch.

I marvel that the sun
Has found its way through tree and leaf.
I marvel that it has gilded
The dying branch with gold.

Jane Horton

Reading Hafiz

Two weeks ago, after a long absence,
I returned to find my garden
Overgrown with weeds and vines.

Each day since, I have pulled up weeds
And cut away the spent, dried blooms
Of the roses, the iris, and the foxglove.

Each morning, looking up from my kitchen table
Into my garden, I think,
"What needs to be done today?

The blowsy, white campanula should be tied up,
The roses fertilized and sprayed.
The butterfly bush has grown too large for its space
And must be moved or pruned."

But this morning I read Hafiz for two hours,
And when I looked up into the garden,
I saw that it was perfect.

Lake   Tatyana Holodnova

Camilla de Nijs

Lost From View

I desire that the spirit be hidden
I desire all poetry to be lost from view
I desire the water to stop running from the spring
And my heart to be like a large rock covered with moss

That our conversation should be the real coin
And its absence like sweet bread still in the oven
That the rattlesnake bake in the sun on ancient red soil trails
And the silence in the eclipsed full moon to be hooted by owls

I can see the lady in the multi-colored coat
Taking care of the dead; the twilight birds sing like bats
I resist the black harvest night bursting into the breathing day
And the bright green fingertips of the Douglas Fir brushing against my skin

But do not forget that everything is here
I can smell a solid presence with my eyes closed
Leave me in my hammock, pondering on how to love
But do not think that anything that is absent will be found there

Camilla de Nijs

Cocoon of Light

Cocoon of light with stars of dust.
The sound of screaming, screeching steel.
Up in the air, exploding glass.
One wheel has hit the restaurant.

The sound of screaming, screeching steel.
The guests get fragments on their food.
One wheel has hit the restaurant.
I love you babe, have fun tonight!

The guests get fragments on their food.
Tattoos are artful scars of ink.
I love you babe, have fun tonight!
That truck is higher on its side.

Tattoos are artful scars of ink.
The doctor says: *We'll airlift her.*
That truck is higher on its side.
The road is dark, just one streetlight.

The doctor says: *We'll airlift her.*
I need a Coke, I want it now.
The road is dark, just one streetlight.
I only see your eyes, mama.

I need a Coke, I want it now.
And God is breathing down my neck.
I only see your eyes, mama.
Cocoon of light with stars of dust.

Francis Knoll

I Watch While I Wait

Before this moment epochs dissolve
Hourglass of moments sift slowly through days
Before my sight, I watch, while I wait.

Present hastens quickly to the past
Churning thoughts stream through the day
Before this moment epochs dissolve.

The wind silently suspends a leaf in the air
Scenes shift, colors change, the day ends
Before my sight, I watch, while I wait.

A life has begun, a life ends
Days are complete while empty and gone
Before this moment epochs dissolve.

Subdividing seconds, an hour has passed
Today a man sips slowly, from his empty bowl
Before my sight, I watch, while I wait.

The thin film of time now bleeds through
Finally diverged, separate and distinct
Before this moment epochs dissolve
Before my sight, I watch, while I wait.

Max   Auguste Haboush

Max Myers

Returning Love

let this moment count as gain
for I have seen your face
and filled with love your gaze is light
as I arise so graced once more

Max Myers

Spring

the swallows returned
is there another sighting
bees humming nearby

Spring Day

this brilliant day clear vibrant
dressed in new spring clothing
yellows and greens and reds
my joy is alive in my chest

here along the road side
soft grasses rising forth
to lay their bed of green
before the soon arrivals

such exciting life
how blessed to see
growing into spring
filled with love's caress

This Day

from my window then
reflecting how the soft gray of winter
has settled all around
clouds low upon the tree tops
damp, still
and here cloaked in warm
pen paper do share
feelings of subtle gratefulness
for this gray winter's day
and the eyes to see

Stefano Petrizzo

On the Way

Walking the path to Chimney Rock.
Beyond the forbidden trails and the cliff edge,
shining buildings of ocean. The wind,
the sky, the spring grasses and wildflowers,
the sea-birds scribbling the air above the water,
the gust in my ears like someone in wet
raingear falling down a stairwell,
all together form a gigantic ball of lint
in the mouth of my head. It is cold.
I am weak and tired. My feet ache
and my ears hurt. Suddenly I find myself
in a silent place, as if someone had shut
all the valves to the sewer of my brain.
I climb up inside myself to this quiet room
and look out a window. It is then I realize
I am walking in God's breath, and I,
my body, and its sufferings are the flags
of nations that no longer exist—
having entered this upper room,
whose walls now fall away and fall apart.

Stefano Petrizzo

He Had Stretched Out from Heaven Shadowing Our Green Lawns

I saw piles of rain feathering the dim light,
and I saw myself seeing it.

Realism was getting in the way, the way the street
crowds around a girl you'd been looking for,

camels and mules and dust and the square
of the marketplace closing around her.

Idealism was undressing my thoughts.
They stood naked in front of Botticelli.

Sometimes I go to other countries by mistake.
It is next year or a hundred years from now

because a flower is bigger than a human being.
If I stopped to count, life would stop.

And I would be alone on a city street
or a Monday morning, and I would wonder

am I making this happen, this whole world,
rain, the picture it took of itself

which I take out of the drawer and set
on the dresser in times of drought.

Going Home   Brian Flynn

Stefano Petrizzo

Blue

The throne in the Boat of Eternity is empty,
the water is still and grey, the wind
is exhausted. There were many people
in different shades of grey trying to get on.
We saw them from behind as they climbed
slowly the wave of hill. While they disappeared
on the other side, remarkable clarity drummed
their senses, fell on them like an invisible
black coat. Their stories were varied: a
shoemaker who wanted to marry, a
retired princess, twelve organ grinders
holding cranks. None were destined to mount
the throne. But what our story doesn't tell
will be misunderstood by the local gang.
Our fetters had rusted by then; breaking off
they shed a fine silt in the sky which some
took to be a blue mist, like when
the crepuscular morning paints the sky,
the trees, the old grey car deep blue,
and you wish you had a shed for all that
color, and you do; if you're very quiet, it will rise.

Stefano Petrizzo

To the Rain

I want to turn to the rain, turn myself inside-out to it,
let it wash my throat and lungs, my naked heart jumping
in the clear puddle on the hard dirt, drop-rings sending out
messages. I want to hear the rain on the shingles of my ears.

The rain will save me, the rain I smell on the wet stones
of my village as the horse clops through the square riderless,
and the rain falls gently on the cap of a peasant entering
the bar to have a caffé, and I turn myself to the rain,

like to my mother, like to the breasts of the south.
I give it everything I have. My eyes are open like hatched birds
flying to the rain. I will give my skin to the rain, like a shroud
the rain washes that soaks it up. I hold it above my mouth,

twist tight and drink in the drops, the dark drops
of my death. I want to catch the rain in my cup.
I will shape myself into a cup to catch the rain.
It is walking over the dead leaves. It fondles the grass

and drips tiny mirrors off a branch, each one a world.
I want the rain to make me clean, to clear my voice
which over time has gathered dirt and grit from sleeping
with sadness, from curling up in corners, grey dirt.

The rain can clean me if I let it, if I strip and give myself, if I give
my mouth and my face and my arms. I will give my penis
to the rain too. I can't hold that back. I must not be afraid.
The rain will be good to it. I will give this poem to the rain.

Pray   Genya Gritchin

Stefano Petrizzo

The Turn

I was thinking of a new model,
the kind you don't think about,
a beginning before the beginning.
But there are no set ways to start
and no set place for the throne of God
once you get there, the floor shining
like a clear mountain lake, the mountain
the only fit symbol for his majesty.
But there's no hiding God behind
symbols, up every morning at 5:00,
he doesn't like missing breakfast,
and he's up all night too, writing
desperate poems, watching movies,
discovering how wonderful it is
to be out of patterns, to be free of 'I'.
God really knows how to relax
in the couch of things, to let them be.
He's not busy being flummoxed
with himself, he has learned
to turn outward, to love things, to turn
away from his Himness, like a star
or a man who puts down the gun
in his mind pointing at himself.
He turns; he lets that train go.
He considers the trees or the cat
Geoffrey, even the clothesline
with its pearls of dew holds something
for him to love. And let's not forget
the light, the morning light, the
evening light, the light as it glimmers
off the gossamer thread cast across

Male Figure   Angela Tuccinardi

his Endlessness, and Space itself
the only room he could fit his large
Infiniteness in without bumping
into something else. And what
could that be outside of God
who is everything? God is God
because he forgot he was God,
forgot about himself and his likeness.
When that happened he realized something
unexpected, when he started to turn
away from himself, he found
that when he really looked
there was nothing that he was not,
and the drops in his beard glistened,
and his hair rose in the wind,
and the sun set on his forehead,
and he found himself then,
more truly and more strange.

Portrait of Gregory Dixon as a Young Boy   Candice Goldman

Candice Goldman

I Want to Run Fast

I want to run fast
I want to sing like a canary
I want to swim far out into the ocean
and be a brave and beautiful girl in love.

I do not want to worry about the stain on the floor in the bathroom
or what time I need to go to bed
or about the two wrinkles on each side of my mouth when I look in the mirror.

I remember the months traveling alone through Mexico
with my little bag holding a bathing suit, some scarves and fifty dollars.
A boyfriend for a week here and a boyfriend for a week there
living the life of the village, the smell of cooking fires and incense in the church
knowing the jungle and its ruins.

I want to feel strong as I walk up the hill to my house
and wake up in the morning eager for what I want and not for what I need to do.
Holding and kissing my grandchildren,
telling them about the time I found an orchid in the jungle as big as my face
while they pretend, dressing themselves up with scarves.

Jeanne Chapman

Paper Dragon

Only at night from the darkest pool of the wood,
That black part, there. Where,
From behind a tree, a corner appears as he
Unfolds himself, gathering dimensions,
And prances big as a house onto the moonlit lawn
Wagging his boxy head.

Patterned in gold and scarlet foil
Dazzling against the night
He lifts one four-clawed paw, and then the next,
Tipping from side to side and blowing
Smoke rings from square nostrils.

He has eyebrows and is
destructively gay.
Behind him a great tail
Thrashes, made of linked triangles
of graduated size.
Trees fall.

I want to be him.
He comes nearer, filling the sky,
opens the hinges of his mouth,
and we both go up
in flame.

Beauregard   Deborah McKay

William Page

The Girl in the Green Dress

The girl in the green dress came
sweeping around my porch today.
With a broom of broken sunlight
and branches she swept the shade away;

with a southern disposition
and a halo of yellow light
she chased away the morning breeze
and the coolness left by the night.

She wished only to be where she was;
she wished only to be sweeping.
She did not know the night's abyss,
or understand the voice of weeping.

She did not know the full moon,
or the sudden swoop of the owl.
She did not know the loneliness
of the coyote's mournful howl.

Barelegged, in a green dress,
with sandals on her feet,
she swept around my porch and left
only the sun's brilliant heat.

She took the morning with her,
and left only the afternoon's glare.
I'll miss the brightness of her eyes
and the wave of her short brown hair.

Lady in Green Shawl   Tatyana Holodnova

I'll miss the way she smiled at me
without having anything to say,
but, most of all, I'll miss the coolness
of the shade she swept away.

William Page

Little Lovers

Two sparrows built their nest in my thoughts last spring.
Little lovers, I asked, have you no place to rest,
has the forest become so desolate and bare
that you cannot find a stout oak for your nest?

"The winter was long," they chirped, as they jumped
and flew among my thoughts, "and the trees
are dressed in black this year, and your thoughts are strong
and pliant and filled with strange memories.

Look how easily a strand of dried grass
and a little mud sits in the branches in your mind."
An army passed through our country last fall.
Is it not terrible? Do you not hate mankind?

Do you not blame those who burned the trees
and deprived you and all the forest birds of spring?
Do you not want to hurt the men who wrecked your home?
How can you be happy? How can you still sing?

"Blame? We cannot blame. We will build our nest
among the branches of your thoughts. What is wrong with that?
Among your ideas there are two suns and a moon
that is always full. What is terrible in that?

We sing because we have each other
and really it is our nature to be happy.
We do not know hate. Is it like the cat?
Does it jump and kill? Can it climb trees?"

It cannot climb trees, but it does kill,
and it is responsible for many terrible crimes.
Its roots are deep and hard to dig out; I know
because I have cut it from my thoughts many times.

Look, the stones at the bottom of my mind are hard.
and far down. Seeing them now makes my heart ache.
If one of your eggs were to fall
I cannot imagine that it would not break.

"Why are you worried? Why should an egg fall?
Our nest will be plenty strong and very high.
Leave us your best thoughts and come back in a month,
and we will be teaching our fledglings to fly."

So I left my thoughts and wandered up
a secluded road far from man's affairs.
That summer I lived in an abandoned barn
with a black he-goat and a speckled mare.

I fed them as if they were human
and learned to live life without thinking.
The three of us understood each other perfectly
and spent our days without once complaining.

And when I returned to collect my thoughts and watch
the little lovers teach their fledglings to fly,
the nest was empty and the sparrows were gone.
By then it was already far into July.

Nude on a Bed   Jonathan Beth

William Page

I Want You to Be Part of My Landscape

I want you to be part of my landscape;
I want my day to begin at your shoulder,
my noon to be lit by your sun,
and my talk to end with your candor.

I want your cool hands to touch
the responsive ground of my skin
with the scattering lightness of fallen leaves;
I want your desire to be my discipline.

I want the distance of my gaze to lounge
with the magnificence of your reclining posture.
I want to see you in profile and in relief,
and to find you in winter and in summer.

I want my art to reveal our intimacy
and our love to be the dress you wear;
I want to entangle my stars in the beautiful
constellation of your fallen hair.

I want the mist of the city's heat
to rise up, to mix with your heavy breathing,
and to enclose my neck and face
with the dark cloud cover of evening.

I want my dusk to settle into the ardor
of your receiving, half-closed eyes
and to feel myself rooted
in the earthly curve of your thighs.

I want the dark perfume of your womb
to become my deep, surrounding night.
Oh who could have imagined the shadow
you would add to my unfolding light?

Who could have foreseen that your flesh
would possess the sudden solitude
of distant cawing crows, who could have foretold
that you would become my drawing, my nude?

Who could have foreseen that our embrace
would become the way I measure my wealth,
or that our love would again and again exhaust
an affirmation that would so quickly renew itself?

William Page

Will and Annihilation

It is because at my back I have
fifty summers of throats calling for water,
mirrors covered with garlands and purple cloth,
the annihilation of rooms brimming
with the bad habits of dead tenants,
the vision of a girl, hot in her summer dress,
who pulls off her hat and tosses her hair back,
and the indiscriminate generosity
of August days giving way to cool nights;
it is because I am sometimes tempted
by the inhospitable craters
of a full moon that seems so pure and so white,
because I have felt something like fear
in the terrible stillness of the stone angel
that is really only a girl with downcast eyes;
it is because, like all men, I am lured
into photographs that are never taken;
and, like all men, have inadvertently become
part of histories that are never told;
it is because annihilation is everywhere
I turn that I use my will to hold back
the prospect of rusted swords, mute telescopes,
the heartache of sickness and age,
and the fear that a star has already burnt
itself out by the time its light reaches me.
I have looked for a will I can take
possession of in the most diverse places:
under thoughts as heavy as rocks,
and beneath emotions as evasive

Robert   Tatyana Holodnova

as a trout startled by the fisherman's lure;
should you ask me, I have to say that I have looked
for a will in the clover's perpetual return,
and inside the bobbing boat of selves
that left me stranded on a green sea
with nothing but the sun at my back and salt water
washing over my bruised and burnt body;
should you ask me, I must admit I have looked
for the will to love under the lemon tree,
on the slanted, peaked roofs of houses
inhabited by good men and women,

and in the river turned muddy and brown
by the pity of the swimmers who never
strayed from the sandy-bottomed shoal
who knew better than to temp the swift
and violent currents by the further bank.
With the color of blue strapped to my back,
I have combed the green wheat and crouched
near my enemies to learn their secrets;
and when the evening darkened the footpaths,
and men wore only the coats of the dead
and the Sunday shoes of their fathers,
and suffered moonless nights without wine,
I stood among them, drank water made bitter
by rusted iron, and was overcome with the joy
that this moment must, like all others, pass away.

It is because I have tasted happiness
that I smile at the naiveté of funeral goers,
and because I have searched my diverse selves
for a will that could unite them that I tolerate
the summer that wraps its fever around me
with the gentleness of palm leaves.

Perhaps I should say it plainly: I have searched
for a will, thinking that it would make me tough
like the lizard's skin or the clay at the bottom
of the waterless pond baked by drought and sun,
but now when the night falls down around me
and the galaxies flow across the dark
like riverbeds of shimmering pebbles,
I allow the self I would have strengthened
to escape from my blistered hands, watch it merge
with the shadows the moon cast among the trees,
and feel how the black distances wash over me.

Alan Burnside

The Gentle Breeze from Home

Woke up this morning, shook myself
There was a fragrance in the air
Reassuring and familiar
Though I couldn't tell you from where
I found myself feeling contented
Like a weight was off my soul
The winds and the storms had relented
I could feel the cool breeze from home

Now I was born near the dunes
And I grew up next to the sea
And I love the music that the sunshine makes
When it dances on the reeds
I love the full moon in August
I love the autumn gales
I love the skylark in April
I love the winter ales

Now I've lived all over this world
And seen many wonderful sights
And known many fine people
Some are still here and some have gone into the night
Did I hear someone whisper,
"My friend, you were never alone"
And were those words carried on
The gentle breeze from home?

Seated Man　　　Angela Tuccinardi

Seated Woman　　　Angela Tuccinardi

Henry Knapp

Taipei, Taiwan

The trees sway gently
In the metallic bustle
Of the city street.

Street traffic roars by.
The snap of an arc welder
Cuts through the chaos.

She runs for the bus,
Blouse billowing and bouncing,
Her breasts bare beneath.

Their dozing heads wave
Like sunflowers in a breeze
As the bus bounces.

Trailing strands of mist,
A giant cloud slowly churns
Over the ridgeline.

Clifford Hook

Going Home

Lead me from the unreal to the real
Deliver me from the belly of the beast
Guide me down the burning staircase
Tongues of fire reaching the sky.

Deliver me from the belly of the beast
Anoint my head with oil
Tongues of fire reaching the sky
Ocean still kisses the sand.

Anoint my head with oil
Gather us unto the promised land
Ocean still kisses the sand
Every end becomes a new beginning.

Gather us unto the promised land
Number our days with wisdom
Every end becomes a new beginning
Each beginning is a place of wonder.

Number our days with wisdom
Lead me from darkness into light
Each beginning is a place of wonder
Stars spinning wheels in the sky.

Lead me from darkness into light
Palm trees near the beach
Stars spinning wheels in the sky
Returning home, just before dark.

Lamp Bearers   Brian Flynn

Palm trees near the beach
A feeling of deep contentment
Returning home, just before dark
Kailua is my place of wonder.

A feeling of deep contentment
The circle brings me home again
Kailua is my place of wonder.
No other place, but here.

Clifford Hook

Ryokan's Gate

Ryokan sits reading, in his home alone
Yesterday he wandered high in the forest
Only friendly clouds and woodcutters come to this area
Keeping his vigil into the night, watching

A sudden snowstorm in May gives him the shivers
New green shoots give hope of spring to Ryokan
Sitting there on heaven's veranda
Going down to the brook for a drink
Always having that simplicity, wherever he may go

This is the life of following the Way
Eternity kisses this flowing through the mirror.

Milena Mlakar

Last Will

When I'll be leaving to a happy hunting ground
all 4 sides of my sky will open
I am clean without confession
no need for church bells, empty words; the truth has set me free

all 4 sides of my sky will open
yet I will accept whatever my angel Death brings
no need for church bells, empty words; the truth has set me free
I've learned so much from silence

yet I will accept whatever my angel Death brings
set me free now, offer ashes to the river—bubbly like me
I've learned so much from silence
yet let me hear the sound of your guitar once more

set me free now, offer ashes to the river—bubbly like me
my life was but a guide map to my simple heart
let me hear the sound of your guitar once more
I have lived and loved enough

my life was but a guide map to my simple heart
dear one, I want you to know
I have lived and loved enough
I believe I'm turning back to star dust

dear one, I want you to know
life is but a Dream Catcher
I believe I'm turning back to star dust
When I'll be leaving to a happy hunting ground

The Cherry Bowl   Agnes Lendech

Milena Mlakar

Blue Tulip

Hold another burning wound, O romantic palm
cooling it down with the help of ice-sharp mind
so that the heart survives

screaming unexpressed
vanished in the dark throat—narrow door
hold another burning wound, O romantic palm

Tomorrow's calling help from above
swaying safely in the arms of gentle shade—blue crown
so that the heart survives

light green longing in his chest for pain fully embraced
a trace of nectar marked his forehead, fleeting triumph
hold another burning wound, O romantic palm

Third day, fragrance of new hope, a breeze of spring
his resurrection blue and pale, complete within a year
so that the heart survives

At last, bundle of memories softly bind with white ribbon
care for life multiplies new roots for joy to come
hold another burning wound, O romantic palm
so that the heart survives

Milena Mlakar

Nothingness

I want to disappear into the nothingness, with my day spilling silver moon
I want twilight to be the scarf around my neck,
my meadow in her evening gown to be the stage, my last performance of the day
Something behind the veil of appearances is swaying, from here to there—into the
nowhere

I want to witness the illusion of this world and my mind slowly losing strength,
I want to feel moist hands and grass beneath my bare feet, my cold forehead,
my hot checks, my dandelions still blooming bright,
faces in the trees and birds chanting (latest) secrets, as if I knew them all . . .

Here, appearances all the same move mysteriously, in slow motion swaying,
losing form, from here to there—into the nowhere
I don't want to turn around; behind my back church bells singing distant warning
to return to my house, to my family, to the world where I belong!

I don't want to be afraid, getting dizzy like today, feeling hypnotized
as if Nothingness invisibly is pulling me away with force
from here to there—into the nowhere
I want to know, if I step into the other side, will I come back again?

Lady with Flower   Genya Gritchin

Fruit Tree   Jonathan Beth

Mohan Vaishnav

Wood's Flowering Moment

The wood in the fall stands in silent toil
Reminiscing the bliss of lovely spring,
Not moaning, nor groaning, but as a foil
For the bright blue sky, untainted and unending.

Does thriving on the quiet strength of belief
That to pass this with patience is the payment
From which it is futile to seek relief,
And to gently wait for the flowering moment?

Though my naïve heart pities the inner autumn,
And yet, doubles its duration and depth
By damning it as the worst lifeless bottom
And not seeing silent submission's worth.

But, as your shade rose in the dark sky of gloom,
Upon its golden foil, fall turned into bloom!

Thoughts of Mary   Kevin Watts

Elisabeth Kehl

Street of Forgiveness

Benevolence is our nature, with charity at its root.

If one withholds the best of oneself
others will perish.

If one withholds the best of oneself
the best of one's Self will die.

Perhaps a shop will be opened
on the quiet street of forgiveness.

It will be a shelter
where ancient truths are told.

It will be a place of experience
burned through sacred tears

where you and I can melt
into nothing

and each other.

Sabina Ayuli

I'm Working for the Gods

I'm working for the gods
Transformation of suffering
Is my work

I have boundaries, too
My gods
I do

But, gods will say,
"Dear, your life is a gift
from us."

I'm working for the gods
Ceasing superiority
Seizing humility
Like contraction and expansion

For the gods
You need not only to attract them,
you need know even more
how to keep them:

I will pursue emptiness
And jump into pain
I will be in peace
And leave in serenity

Till Dawn   Takayuki Harada

Man in a Turban   Jonathan Beth

Julian Branston

Meeting a Poem
for Stanley Fligner

A man reads a poem
and finishing the last line
leaves at once for a merchant ship
carrying all that he owns in a duffel bag
and returning many years later
burned by the sun, one eye scorched out by a pirate's bullet
his bag full of opals
he gives out that rare warmth
of someone who has endured incredible hardship
and discovered his own heroism

However, the poem that he read
exhausted
retires to a small nursing home in Bournemouth
comforted only by the distant sound of the lifting, swelling tide
and the social sounds
of light chat and sweet jokes
that it could not comprehend
but which warmed it anyway

Which is the fate
of some poems

Other poems survive, abandoned
like the Hebridean rocks
that no one visits
except sneering seagulls, violent impartial winds
and the black sheep on their tops
who look rusty after the sun gets to them

Other poems
break into your house
and sample everything that delights you:
The classic crust of cream on top of the milk bottle
Low, sinuous jazz recordings
That spot that you always notice but never see
of the key hidden under the plant pot
The inside of a pajama arm
Your secret pile of fluff from the dryer filter
The number of sips left in your thirty-year old Courvoisier
Special books where only your thumb may serve as a bookmark
While in your driveway, there's always the special sound of the gravel
on your walking shoe
These and other empathies this poem steals from you
and if you defend them—and they have no value but their experience—
the poem's intervention, which might have gone unnoticed,
becomes pillage and arson, ransacking your life for what you mean
in every single secret corner

Other poems undress you
specifically to make each nakedness
a removal to that burning utmost
where desire meets the undercarriage of surrender;
when the draught of pleasure pours into the vessel of thwarted recognition,
so that even an intimacy in the moment
becomes a trademark of the past
or when the glowing significance of your identity
becomes an enigmatic reference that may never be found

Then there are poems that shape a place in which to sit
and there to watch the world,
giving up to unknown rhythms
treating the exotic as a tenant in the room above your head
charging rent, enduring the larger-than-life parties and monumental lovemaking

yet secretly pleased to be greeted
by this goofy enthusiast
all the while knowing that a tenant is really a visitor
and you the port
where ships trade for a place to stay
and wait for a time to go

Then there are thwarted poems
bleeding quietly in their prisons and confinements
disfigured by the outer layer that keeps them in
dying from barely engaged interest
of prison clothes and vapid slops

Until one day and every day
above the concrete windows and metal grills
a minstrel song rises
and the rays of the sun
suddenly pour in like a melody

Pretty as a Picture

Museo Capitolino. Nicoletta stepped down the museum stairs then walked a block to the bus-stop. And again, as always, that same deflated feeling came over her. How could just two hours in the art gallery make the world look so different? And why did it have to be that the world always came up lacking, that the world seemed second best? The world in the paintings were so wonderfully ordered. Its buildings were arranged skillfully, their best features on display, all the best was brought pleasingly to the fore. Flowers, bushes and trees, lakes and forests, clouds and mountains—all were selected and displayed with such sensitive intention, their colors combined in the most enchanting ways possible.

In the museum she had wandered happily from one room to another, met and cheered on all sides by harmonious scenes. Back here on the street, though, not one thing was cheerful. Nothing inside her could greet *this* world with the same open arms. A tree was a tree in both worlds, and a cloud was a cloud and a building a building. But everything in this real world looked forlorn and haphazard, and seemed sadly neglected. Here were the same Roman *palazzi* she had just seen in the pictures, only these had had drain-pipes, antennae and electric wires, and storefronts with garish signs. The few trees she could see were in scraggly half-health, disposed here and there looking lost, disarrayed. As for the sky—just a simple flat blue—it was there. Not much else could said. Yes, this Rome was a poor double of the Rome in the pictures; it seemed everywhere random, diminished, banal.

Most dismaying of all were the people. In the paintings all were costumed and bejeweled, posed and composed, their every gesture calculated to the last expressive detail. And if the finery was wonderful, even better were the figures, so lavishly robed, or best of all, nude. What pleasure she took from the graceful posture of a woman's nakedness, or the sinewy muscle of the well-formed man's. Best of all was the body's summit, its crown: the human head. Heads with compelling physiognomies and spiritual faces, embedded eyes shining brightly with silent revelation.

What rude decline then, to these motley commuters, waiting beside her at the bus-stop in ungainly repose. From the curbside she surveyed them as they stood against the graffiti'd wall with its tattered posters. She found herself forcibly being reminded of something… what was it? Of a police line-up? No, that was not quite it. Yes—now she knew—it was a psychiatric ward, where each was an unknowing caricature, a grotesque imitation—of himself. Here were no proud bodies expressive of noble interiors, but just slouched ones, resigned and crooked ones, stuffed ones, compacted ones, abandoned ones. Here were no searching eyes, no questing spark or nascent feelings. These eyes were heavy-lidded or vacant, or wistful or suspicious, or fearful or dead. To be sure, waiting for a bus in the sun does not bring out one's best. But apart from this circumstance, she was seeing the foundation, she knew. And it was empty and ugly, and made her sober and sad.

Samuel   Susan Goldman

What a hoax were all these pictures and statues, with their shopworn Greek symmetries! They were fantasy, nothing more: teasing hints of ideals that had no real existence save in the gilded frames of museums. If art mirrored life, then that was not art she had seen in the museum. Surely *this* was art instead, looming above her this very moment: this poster selling jeans. The figures in the poster were bigger than any she had ever seen in a painting. And this poster was clearly valuable, housed in a frame made of steel that had night lights and protective glass. The reason for this considerable structure was to present the Jeans Man and Jeans Woman, figures quite as popular as Christ and the Madonna.

Wearing jeans but no shirt, the man's prize-fighter torso was flexed to maximum relief, captured in full *chiaroscuro* by some able photographer. His thug's face was brutish. His eyes stared out like a predator. His lips were curled in a sneer. His jaw sprouted stubble. His hair was disordered. The Old Masters, she thought, would have known better where to put him. He was wasted in this jeans ad; he belonged in a painting. He should be Cain by the fire, devouring his slain brother's lamb. Or the soldier, plate in hand, with the Baptist's severed head. Or the son who scornfully mocked wise old Noah's naked loins. Or just another face in the crowd that was hungry for a crucifixion.

His consort in the poster wore jeans just as he did. Her torso was unclothed also. But while his chest was bared fully, hers was half hidden beneath her carefully crossed arms, while her bold coy lidded eyes looked out teasingly, from above. She too would have her place in the paintings of the Masters. She would be Salome. Or maybe Potiphar. Or a sybarite at Gomorrah. Or the woman at whom none were sufficiently pure to cast the first stone. What good was a museum, wondered Nicoletta, if it cast her into dark thoughts like these? What good was an ideal world, that was devoured so quickly by the real?

A tall Ethiopian woman walked up to the bus-stop and took her place at the grafitti'd wall. Nicoletta was drawn at once to her fine native garb. Folds of brightly colored fabric fell gracefully from her shoulders to her womanly broad hips, which were tilted in classic *contrapposta*, as she surely did not know. These folds were gathered at her waist by a bright scarlet sash which then loosed them on downwards in cascades to her feet. Quite like the toga Nicoletta had just moments ago been looking at, in the museum. Only now it was better, incomparably better. For this was no toga of stone or white paint in some dreamed-up Roman scene. It was real, with its happy hues keyed perfectly with the bright summer sky. This woman wore a turban, too, and that too was bright and happy. But best of all, better than all of this—was her round mocha face and her plain open features, all patience and modesty, calm and benign.

Nicoletta felt content now to linger at this curbside—with this tall noble woman with the calm mocha face, so pleasing and bright against the fine summer sky. And such a fine sky it was, Nicoletta noticed, quite suddenly. So shimmery and sunny, so boundless and blue. The longer she gazed upon this dark toga'd woman, the brighter the sun seemed to blaze, the more boundless became the sky.

How lovely were the sun's rays, now showering hot unseen light. Light that showered down on everything, and everywhere, and always: before these noisy cars, these dirty buildings, before this city, before even herself. Words formed in her mind unbidden: *Phaeton. Helios. Amun-Ra.* Light's beauty showered down everywhere, profligate, indiscriminate, bathing smoggy streets filled with traffic. Bathing skewed bodies at a bus-stop. Washing buildings free of signs and wires. Washing everything new, fresh and clean. Everything overwhelmed by it. Everything now clothed in its true timeless raiment. Nicoletta now saw today's Rome as she knew it in her heart, but had briefly forgotten.

It was pretty as a picture.

Alastair MacDonald

Natural Heaven

In the calm, leafy glade,
and the quiet, cooling shade,
glides the inviting stream, shimmering
soothing, rushing and murmuring.

As I look up, the sun flash-dazzles through the canopy given
my self there, at peace and divine, in this natural heaven
Cadzow Park, Hamilton, Lanarkshire, Scotland, July 2011

Tzvi Shmilovich

I'll Enter

You, the hot, slender milk and honey one
I'll enter you through an inviting port
at about your Tel-Aviv-Jaffa waist.
Sneak inside your Jerusalem
along the Burma road.
Poke your treasures, wander the alluring alleys
mount your church-prickled mount of olives.
Peek down your back side—
the russet, rough, arid Judea-desert.
Descend its abrupt slopes
into your winking Jericho basin.
Be slapped hard by the dry heat.
Feel your obstinate Masada prominence
its titillating resistance opposite
the blue dead seascape;
lick your salty scorching air.
Snake down your drip-systems strewn Arava depression.
At about the land's hips
Squeeze your bright sandy Negev
till the Eilat toes twirl and curl
in the Eilat sand
while they're gently lapped by the Red-Sea waves
lightly scraped by its colored corals
nibbled by its tiny fishes.
Your north'll cool us a bit.
Pause to sample the fruity flesh
of your appetizing fertile valleys.
Play your sweet fiddle-like lake. Make miracles by it.
Press against the Galilee mountain tops,
the Tabor roundness,

The Binding of Isaac   YoHana Bat Adam

be tickled by the tips of the Nazareth churches,
especially the onion-domed Russian Orthodox one.
Be chilled in the coolness breezing from the Lebanon white heights.
Join your Carmel incline gracefully dropping into the ocean.
Then supine on your beaches soak up the sun.
Probe your Carmel wadis
Love your mystic caves
inside you I forgo history
can go extinct vanish
like the Neanderthal.

Tzvi Shmilovich

March in the Sierra Foothills

The black cat's perched
lordly on top of the rail's weathered wood deck
in the silvery mist.
The railing shows holes
like an old redneck's mouth.

The encircling ring of the manzanita brush,
Hunched and twisted bewitches through the fog
glares at the lawn, at us, the invaders.
The skeletal yellow chair
paint peeling, abandoned on the grass.

Opposite this—
the glowing fireplace
and the third glass filled
with the thick Red.

Tzvi Shmilovich

Not This Way Nor That

No, you won't take the cure of the stone,
Bleed your world into an end-all creed
Nor seek solace in graces of foam.

You won't drain yourself into a phantom,
Waste away dodging the aches of the need.
No, you won't take the relief of the stone

Nor lash at itches that don't leave you alone.
Mature lusts know you must pay to abscond
But you won't be becalmed by embraces of foam.

When the envelope's used, crumbled or torn
Some glut in denying the hungers their food;
You—cannot take the way of the stone

Take shelter, shut out the storm.
You invite the tempest, the torment of want;
You won't seek solace in embraces of foam.

Prescribed bubbles won't drown your common,
nagging, worldly, blustery appetite;
No, you won't take the cure of the stone
Nor seek solace in graces of foam.

Self–Portrait   Genya Gritchin

Tzvi Shmilovich

My Multitudes

"…I contain multitudes."
"Apart from the pulling and the hauling stands what I am."

Walt Whitman

Mine scatter over great distances,
hop in the fog on slippery cliffs, butt heads,
lock horns, goad each other; follow impossible trails, fall.
And the standing-apart thing bucks.

Once we were awed by the Grand Central scene;
watched how the chaos merges into rivulets
weaves into streams, en masse
is delivered to its respective slots.

If only such a scheme could be applied
to my crowd, if not tame, at least manage the lot.
But we can only do what we did there sometimes
having nowhere in particular to go, a bit tipsy each time,

amidst the afternoon rush come suddenly to a standstill—
a pocket of disruption midstream like a raised finger
pointing, lift the head, look up
at the painted ceiling.

.

www.ingramcontent.com/pod-product-compliance
Lightning Source LLC
Chambersburg PA
CBHW040823050726
47507CB00021B/112